YOUR KNOWLEDGE HAS VALUE

- We will publish your bachelor's and master's thesis, essays and papers

- Your own eBook and book - sold worldwide in all relevant shops

- Earn money with each sale

Upload your text at www.GRIN.com and publish for free

Bibliographic information published by the German National Library:

The German National Library lists this publication in the National Bibliography; detailed bibliographic data are available on the Internet at http://dnb.dnb.de .

This book is copyright material and must not be copied, reproduced, transferred, distributed, leased, licensed or publicly performed or used in any way except as specifically permitted in writing by the publishers, as allowed under the terms and conditions under which it was purchased or as strictly permitted by applicable copyright law. Any unauthorized distribution or use of this text may be a direct infringement of the author s and publisher s rights and those responsible may be liable in law accordingly.

Imprint:

Copyright © 2018 GRIN Verlag
Print and binding: Books on Demand GmbH, Norderstedt Germany
ISBN: 9783668715899

This book at GRIN:

https://www.grin.com/document/426888

Oluwagbenga Afolabi

Facebook Security Breach. Security Risk Analysis and Recommendation

GRIN Verlag

GRIN - Your knowledge has value

Since its foundation in 1998, GRIN has specialized in publishing academic texts by students, college teachers and other academics as e-book and printed book. The website www.grin.com is an ideal platform for presenting term papers, final papers, scientific essays, dissertations and specialist books.

Visit us on the internet:

http://www.grin.com/

http://www.facebook.com/grincom

http://www.twitter.com/grin_com

Saint Leo University

Term Paper

On Facebook Security Policy

By

Oluwagbenga Michael Afolabi

Strategic Planning Cybersecurity (MBA 590)

April 16, 2018

Abstract

Facebook has revolutionized the way people (End-users) communicate with peers and close relatives, these users share personal information with Facebook. The platform, in turn, uses these users' information to match them with other users who share similarities in information through algorithms. The primary focus of this paper is on the security implications of users sharing their personal information on Facebook. Additionally, we will examine the recent data security breach on Facebook involving Cambridge analytical and its implication for Facebook and other data mining entities. The analysis will examine the loophole exploited by third-party apps to gain elevated access to users and sub-user data. We also want to establish if Facebook is taken appropriate steps to safeguard user information by following the federal trade commission guidelines in protecting user information.

Introduction

Facebook (www.facebook.com) is the brainchild of then Harvard undergraduate Mark Zuckerberg, the social platform was founded in 2004 (Facebook, 2018). The platform is an integration of different sites that was primarily focused around colleges, users who wish to create an account to use their college uniform resource locator or URL (@college.edu), to register on the platform. Facebook presently boosts of about 1.86billion users making it the biggest online social platform in the world. Users who create a profile on Facebook submit their data to Facebook after agreeing to its Acceptable Use Policy (AUP). The user information allows Facebook to match the user with other profile based on the user's information. Additionally, such user data are also allowing Facebook to update the user's news feed and suggestions that correlates with the user's profile data.

To ensure the platform free and meet is debt obligations, the user data is used by Facebook to tailor advertisement to these users. What makes Facebook indispensable to other entities is its wealth of user data that can be used to micro target users per their activities and information on the site. Per its website, Facebook collects user information, their activities on and off the site, location, device location, hardware, software, Connection information such as the name of your mobile operator or ISP, browser type, mobile phone number, IP address, etc. In 2007, Facebook opened its platform to third-party apps with the objectives of increasing customer experience and return on investment. Additionally, the introduction of third-party allows users to play games, play quizzes, shop, and use dating apps on Facebook. However, to protect user information, and comply with the Federal Trade Commission Act Section 5, called the "unfair or deceptive act " (ICLG, n. d).

Background

Facebook ensures users accept its term of use policy before the user can access its platform. The opening up of Facebook to third-party applications has increased the firm's return on investment. In the words of Facebook founder Mark Zuckerberg, "Until now, social networks have been closed platforms. Today, we're going to end that," (Pierson D., 2018). However, the opening up of Facebook to third-party application introduced a new kind of security policy concern for Facebook. It raises the concern regarding the amount of data access and privilege these third-party applications has over user data. For the proper analysis of these security concerns, we will examine the firm's security policies that relate to how third parties access or the level of privilege an application has over user data.

Facebook employs the Hyper Preprocessor (PHP) a server-side script which it uses to format the services it renders on its platform. Facebook in its early days stores its data in a central server, however, with the advancement in cloud technologies, the firm has migrated to cloud storage by storing its data at different data farms. The firm's massive data infrastructure must seamlessly to ensure user satisfaction while on its platform. "Before it started building its own server farms, Facebook managed its infrastructure by leasing "wholesale" data center space from third-party landlords" (datacenterknowledge.com, 2010).

Social Networking

Social Networking application/platforms: Social Networking application/platforms like Facebook allow users to share their information on its platform via the user's profile. Such information includes the user's pictures, contact information, lifestyle, activities, and interest. The advantage of Facebook above other social networking site is its algorithm that allows users to be matched with friends based on the information those users provide will registering on its platform.

Information stored on Facebook: Facebook collect and store information about users, this information includes;

- Things you do on Facebook and information a user share on its platform
- Information from friends on their activities and the information they provide
- Information about payments
- User device information
- Information from websites visited by users and
- Information from third-party applications and partners.

These information is used by Facebook to Communication with users, the information is also used to show and measure advertisement and services on its platforms, and promote safety and security.

How Facebook share user information: Facebook share Non-Personally Identifiable Information Only with third-party, such third-party include advertising, measurement and Analytics Services. The user information is also shared with vendors, service providers, and partners.

Statement of Rights and Responsibilities

The statement of rights and responsibilities (SRR) is the terms of services between Facebook and those that interact with the Facebook platform. The purpose of an SRR is to inform users of how their data are been used by Facebook. The SRR inform users of their privacy rights including the right users have regarding the information they share on the platform. For instance, a subsection of the policy states the user grants Facebook a "non-exclusive, transferable, sub-licensable, royalty-free, worldwide license to use any IP content that you post on or in connection with Facebook (IP License)"(Facebook, n. d). The Statement of Rights and Responsibilities also inform users about their privileges on the platform, it informs users of what content users can post on the platform, what information users can collect on Facebook. The term of service also prohibits the use of automated means in mining user data. It states, "You will not collect users' content or information, or otherwise access Facebook, using automated means (such as harvesting bots, robots, spiders, or scrapers) without our prior permission" (Facebook, n. d).

Data Policy

The Facebook Data policy inform users of the types of information that is being collected by Facebook, such information includes the user location, photos, the date a file was created. Information about how the service is being used e.g. the type of content users view on Facebook, information others provide on the user, the user's network connections, payment information, device information including; operating system, device location, software name and type, etc. Facebook data policy also inform users that it collects information about third-party websites and applications visited by the user and how such information is used. Section III, subsection III of the Facebook Data privacy policy addresses how third-party application access user data and the level of access to user information by the third-party application. The policy states that:

> Apps, websites and third-party integrations on or using our Services. When you use third-party apps, websites or other services that use, or are integrated with, our Services, they may receive information about what you post or share. For example, when you play a game with your Facebook friends or use the Facebook Comment or Share button on a website, the game developer or website may get information about your activities in the game or receive a comment or link that you share from their website on Facebook. In addition, when you download or use such third-party services, they can access your Public Profile, which includes your username or user ID, your age range and country/language, your list of friends, as well as any information that you share with them. Information collected by these apps, websites or integrated services is subject to their terms and policies (Facebook, 2016).

Analysis of Security Policies

The Facebook security policies show that the firm pays more emphasis on securing its platform from malicious actors by using different countermeasures to mitigate risk to it information infrastructures. However, this research work is focuse on its security policy and how it affects the end users. Information security policies can only be effective when there is a management buy-in. In 2011, Facebook settled a case with the FTC for deceiving customers that Users' private information on its platform will remain private. However, the firm allows third-party applications from other users (friends list) access that information. "Facebook promised users that it would not share their personal information with advertisers. It did"(ftc.gov, 2011).

In 2018, Facebook claimed that Cambridge Analytical has illegally harvested fifty million of its user data, however, it was later discovered that rather, eighty-seven million users' data were compromised (Romano, A., 2018). The analysis of the breach shows that between the two-years period (2013 to 2015), the firm Cambridge Analytical was able to harvest the profile information of eighty million users without informing the users that their data has been harvested. The data which is then used to strategically target users based on their interest, personality, and other information on the user's profile. Additionally, the firm used this data to shape the recently concluded United States Presidential election.

Per reports on the news media, Cambridge Analytical was able to utilize a loophole in the Application Programming Interface (API) of Facebook (Romano, A., 2018). This loophole allows third-party applications to harvest data of users on their application and that of their friends. To effectively analyze the security policy of Facebook, this research will be based on the completeness and thoroughness of its security policy, compliance with recognized industry, government, and regulatory standards.

Completeness/Thoroughness: The Facebook security policies covers a broad spectrum of its Information infrastructure. Its security policies cover Acceptable Use policy which the firm labeled "Statement of Right and Responsibilities". Additionally, the firm has a data security policy, Adverting policies, The Facebook Platform Policy which covers the framework of third-party application should be built, including its data privacy. The third-party application on Facebook allows users to play online games, take surveys, and placement of advertisement to mention a few. Furthermore, the firm Self-Serve Ads Terms, serves as an extension of the Statement of Rights and Responsibilities. It covers the Terms of Agreement between Facebook and any third-party advertisement and application. The Terms of Agreement is also governed by the Facebook Data Policy, Community Payments Terms.

Compliance: Information system and user data are governed by different rules and regulations, some of these rules and regulation include:

The Privacy Act of 1974; the act "establishes a code of fair information practices that govern the collection, maintenance, use, and dissemination of information about individuals that is maintained in a system of records by federal agencies" (Doj, 2015).

The Federal Trade Commission Act; Section 5(a) prohibits the unfair deceptive acts or practices in or affecting commerce. It also covers the protection of consumer data security. The act also applies to the Fair Debt Collection Practices Act and the Telemarketing and Consumer Fraud and Abuse Prevention Act. These regulations outline how firms collect, store, and use customer information on its platform. Besides the Federal Trade Commission Act, there is barely any other regulation guiding the use and protection of user data on social network in the United States. This point as brought to light at the recent congressional and Senate hearing regarding the unauthorized harvesting on the Facebook user data in 2016.

However, on May 2018, the European Union introduced a new rules and regulations guiding the use of European citizen by social network platform.

> As of May 2018, with the entry into application of the General Data Protection Regulation, there is one set of data protection rules for all companies operating in the EU, wherever they are based. Stronger rules on data protection mean; people have more control over their personal data businesses benefit from a level playing field (ec.europa.eu, 2018).

> In accordance with the European Union General Data Protection Regulation (GDPR), any European Union resident using any electronic media information must meet its guidelines. The modified law states that user data can be transferred outside the European Union on if the European Union determines that the receiving party ensure appropriate and adequate level protection of such data. Additionally, such data must be in consent with the user/ owner of the data before such data is transferred. The GDPR also mandate these platforms to promptly notify users in the event of a data breach which may result in the infringement of the right and freedom of such individual. In the event of non-compliance by such a firm, a fine of twenty million Euro or four percent of total global revenue will be levied on such entity.

Results

Our investigation of the breach of Facebook security policy shows that this breach stems from a spectrum of several lapses both in the firm's security policies, in the firm's business practices, and its organizational culture. During the early years of Facebook, a research was conducted by Harvey Jones and Jose Hiram Soltren in 2005. The report found that Facebook has deceived users regarding how it uses the data provided by users. Also, the report found that Facebook its early days allow the harvesting of its data by third parties. For instance, the researchers were able to conduct a web crawler search on the platform to mine users' information. Although Facebook has since prohibited the use of such tools on its website, the gap in security persists.

Furthermore, Facebook was made to pay a fine to the Federal Trade Commission (FTC) in 2011, the firm was accused of lying to its customers by making privacy promises that it did not keep. Some of the charges include an allegation that Facebook overrides user's privacy settings by making it public. The firm was also accused of lying to users that its applications would only have access to the data it needed to operate however, the application can view all user data. The firm also promised not to share user information with a third-party advertisement, the firm also made user data available to third-party applications used by their friends. In 2018, it was reported that Cambridge Analytical through a researcher created a quiz application that was installed by 300,000 users. However, the application was able to gain access to this user's information and that of their friends, at the end of the day, eighty-seven million users' information was mined via this application. This bears a close similarity to the incident that happened in 2011 alluded to earlier.

In analyzing the firm's security policies and Statement of Rights and Responsibilities (Acceptable Use Policy), the policies show some loophole in security policy that can be exploited by these third-party applications. For instance, a section of its Data security states that:

> When you download or use such third-party services, they can access your Public Profile, which includes your username or user ID, your age range and country/language, your list of friends, as well as any information that you share with them. Information collected by these apps, websites or integrated services is subject to their terms and policies (Facebook, 2016).

This section of the security policy imply that third-party applications has full privileged access to users' information and such data cannot be recalled by the Facebook once it leaves its platform. The implication of this is that in the event of a breach to its security policy, by a third-party application, such information cannot not be retrieved by Facebook per its Data Policy.

The analysis of the Facebook Policies also shows that although the firm did not comply with applicable laws, these policies are not enforced by the organization and the firm is not making any concerted efforts to ensure compliance by these third-party applications. Furthermore, our analysis shows that the firm is also exploiting this same loophole to increase its return on investment by claiming ignorance even after being fined by the Federal Trade Commission for similar incident.

Additionally, the use of the internet is growing at an exponential rate and the regulations governing the use of user's information has not been able to catch up with this fast pace. Therefore, such lapses have allowed firm's like Facebook to continually exploit this gap in policy formulation to trade on Users' information without strong retribution from the government. It is an organization's responsibility to oversight what information a vendor or third party can access and the level of authority granted to such third-party company.

To comply with the Gramm-Leach-Bliley Act, a bank is responsible for the protection of a customer's financial information, the bank is also responsible when a vendor view/ or process such information (Johnson, R., 2015). Therefore, it is an organization's responsibility to monitor access to user information by employees and third parties in accordance with the law. Such compliance ensure risk to the data access is minimized and the firm is not expensing resources on fines by regulatory bodies. To this end, Facebook Data policy shows that proper security policy is not in place to protect user information outside its network.

The Cambridge analytical data breach also shows that the firm does not have an effective Incident Response Team and Incident Response Plan or the firm decided against activating its IRT immediately the incident was discovered. Furthermore, the firm failed to inform its users on time about the data breach nor has the firm made any concerted effort to mitigate reoccurrence of such incident, if it has, it is yet to be seen. Public records show that this practice has been going on at Facebook from its inception therefore, it is part of its strategic objective to allow such attack vector to exist in its data policy. However, we believe the recent disaster that occasioned the revelation of the data harvesting and the subsequent appearance by Mack Zuckerberg at the House and Senate hearing will prompt the company to make necessary changes to its data policy and its revenue generation strategy without altering its bottom-line in the long-run.

Recommendations

The analysis of Facebook security policies shows a pervasive control weakness due to the reoccurrence of the same vulnerability in Facebook security policy. Therefore, we recommend the following actionable step be taken by Facebook to mitigate these loopholes in its security policies.

Change its Data Security policy: This research shows that third-party application has on several occasions exploited the loophole in the data security policy of Facebook to harvest and use such data as they please without any control from Facebook. Therefore, a new data policy must allow Facebook oversight on how this data is being used after they leave the Facebook platform and Facebook reserve the right to recall such data in the event it is used for unlawful purposes.

User Awareness: It is the responsibility of Facebook to make users aware directly or specify that third-party applications inform users on the privilege that they (users) grant such application on its platform through its Facebook platform policy. Additionally, Facebook must inform users when their information has been compromised by an attacker or third-party application.

Access control Implementation: It is imperative that third-party application must not gain access to personal information of Users except with the consent of such user (s). Also, such user's consent must be sought before access is granted. Therefore, Facebook must implement access control that escalate a third-party's access privilege to all of user's personal data and that of the user's friends list. Such right must only be granted to its Administrators.

Deleted account: Facebook must ensure that user account that has been deleted, the user data must not be accessed by a third-party application and by Facebook except under legal requirements. The firm must also ensure it comply with the United States Safe Harbor Framework governing data transfer between two platforms. The "Safe Harbor is the name of an agreement between the United States Department of Commerce and the European Union that regulated the way that U.S. companies could export and handle the personal data of European citizens" (Rouse, M., n. d). The stipulate that companies provide a symmetric method of transferring data across the border of participating countries and such firms must inform users that such personal data are being gathered.

Third-party Privacy audit: Facebook must also ensure it obtain privacy audit from a third-party application that meet the Federal Trade Commission framework and must ensure it verifies the security of third-party applications.

Summary

It is imperative for firms to recognize the effect reputational damage can have on its objectives. Furthermore, noncompliance with laws and regulations can lead to lawsuits, fines and scrutiny from users and regulators. Therefore, to mitigate such blow backs, Facebook must craft a security policy that cover the spectrum of the recommendation of this research and beyond. The advantage of such move by Facebook allows it to restore its lost confidence with users and regulatory authorities like the Federal Trade commission.

References

datacenterknowledge.com, (2010). The Facebook Data Center FAQ. Retrieved from: http://www.datacenterknowledge.com/data-center-faqs/facebook-data-center-faq

Doj, (2015). Privacy Act of 1974. Retrieved from: https://www.justice.gov/opcl/privacy-act-1974

ec.europa.eu, 2018). 2018 reform of EU data protection rules. Retrieved from: https://ec.europa.eu/commission/priorities/justice-and-fundamental-rights/data-protection/2018-reform-eu-data-protection-rules_en

Facebook, (2016). Data Policy. Retrieved from: https://www.facebook.com/about/privacy/

Facebook, (n. d). Statement of Rights and Responsibilities. Retrieved from: https://www.facebook.com/legal/terms

ftc.gov, (2011). Facebook Settles FTC Charges That It Deceived Consumers By Failing To Keep Privacy Promises. Retrieved from: https://www.ftc.gov/news-events/press-releases/2011/11/facebook-settles-ftc-charges-it-deceived-consumers-failing-keep

ICLG, (n. d). Relevant Legislation and Competent Authorities. Retrieved from: https://iclg.com/practice-areas/data-protection/data-protection-2017/usa

Johnson, R., (2015). Security policies and Implementation Issues (2nd ed). Burlington, MA: Jones & Bartlett Learning. ISBN: 978-1-284-05599-3

Pierson D., (2018). Facebook needed third-party apps to grow. Now it's left with a privacy crisis. Retrieved from: http://www.latimes.com/business/technology/la-fi-tn-facebook-third-parties-20180320-story.html

Romano, A., (2018). The Facebook data breach wasn't a hack. It was a wake-up call. Retrieved from: https://www.vox.com/2018/3/20/17138756/facebook-data-breach-cambridge-analytica-explained

YOUR KNOWLEDGE HAS VALUE

- We will publish your bachelor's and master's thesis, essays and papers

- Your own eBook and book - sold worldwide in all relevant shops

- Earn money with each sale

Upload your text at www.GRIN.com
and publish for free